Isaac Asimov's

21st Century

Library of the
Universe

The Solar System

# Mercury

BY ISAAC ASIMOV

WITH REVISIONS AND UPDATING BY RICHARD HANTULA

Gareth Stevens Publishing
A WORLD ALMANAC EDUCATION GROUP COMPANY

Please visit our web site at: www.garethstevens.com
For a free color catalog describing Gareth Stevens Publishing's list of high-quality
books and multimedia programs, call 1-800-542-2595 (USA) or 1-800-387-3178 (Canada).
Gareth Stevens Publishing's fax: (414) 332-3567.

Library of Congress Cataloging-in-Publication Data

Asimov, Isaac.
    Mercury / by Isaac Asimov; with revisions and updating by Richard Hantula.
       p. cm. – (Isaac Asimov's 21st century library of the universe. The solar system)
    Rev. ed. of: Nearest the sun: the planet Mercury. 1995.
    Summary: Describes the planet closest to the sun, examining its size and composition,
its surface features, its orbit, and efforts to learn more about this planet.
    Includes bibliographical references and index.
    ISBN 0-8368-3237-X (lib. bdg.)
    1. Mercury (Planet)–Juvenile literature. [1. Mercury (Planet).] I. Hantula, Richard.
II. Asimov, Isaac. Nearest the sun: the planet Mercury. III. Title. IV. Isaac Asimov's 21st
century library of the universe. Solar system.
    QB611.A76   2002
    523.41–dc21                  2002066808

JJ 523.41

This edition first published in 2002 by
**Gareth Stevens Publishing**
A World Almanac Education Group Company
330 West Olive Street, Suite 100
Milwaukee, WI 53212 USA

Series editor: Betsy Rasmussen
Cover design and layout adaptation: Melissa Valuch
Picture research: Matthew Groshek
Additional picture research: Diane Laska-Swanke
Production director: Susan Ashley

The editors at Gareth Stevens Publishing have selected science author Richard Hantula to bring
this classic series of young people's information books up to date. Richard Hantula has written
and edited books and articles on science and technology for more than two decades. He was
the senior U.S. editor for the *Macmillan Encyclopedia of Science*.

In addition to Hantula's contribution to this most recent edition, the editors would like to
acknowledge the participation of two noted science authors, Greg Walz-Chojnacki and
Francis Reddy, as contributors to earlier editions of this work.

Printed in the United States of America

1 2 3 4 5 6 7 8 9 06 05 04 03 02

# Contents

We live in an enormously large place — the Universe. It is only natural that we would want to understand this place, so scientists and engineers have developed instruments and spacecrafts that have told us far more about the Universe than we could possibly imagine.

We have seen planets up close, and spacecrafts have even landed on some. We have learned about quasars and pulsars, super-novas and colliding galaxies, and black holes and dark matter. We have gathered amazing data about how the Universe may have come into being and how it may end. Nothing could be more astonishing.

Scientists know less about Mercury than any other planet in our Solar System, except for remote Pluto. One reason for this is that Mercury is so close to the Sun that it is usually over-whelmed by the Sun's light when we try to observe it. Another reason is that it has been visited by only one space probe — *Mariner 10*. Still, scientists have been able to gather many surprising details about this small celestial body that moves the fastest of all the planets.

• Mercury •

Mercury's rough, cratered
surface resembles
the Moon's.

# Small, Yet Mighty

Mercury is a small planet. At 3,032 miles (4,879 kilometers) in diameter, it is only about 3/8 the width of Earth. Mercury is the closest planet to the Sun — only 36 million miles (57.9 million km) away on the average. Its orbit takes it as close as 28.6 million miles (46 million km) to the Sun. This is almost 70 percent closer to the Sun than Earth gets.

The surface of any planet this close to the Sun is bound to get very hot — as hot as 850° Fahrenheit (450° Centigrade). This is hot enough to melt lead.

Since Mercury is so close to the Sun, the Sun's gravity pulls hard. Earth orbits the Sun at 18.5 miles (29.78 km) a second, but Mercury orbits at an average of 29.75 miles (47.9 km) a second. It is the "quickest" of all the planets in the Solar System.

*Left:* Glowing streams of molten metal pour into molds at a foundry. The surface of Mercury gets hot enough to melt lead.

# A Day Longer Than a Year?

From our point of view on Earth, Mercury has an unusual relationship with the Sun. Its closeness to the Sun gives it a small orbit. It moves so quickly that its trip around the Sun – one Mercury year – takes only 88 days. Mercury, however, turns very slowly on its axis, so the time from sunrise to sunrise – one Mercury day – is 176 Earth days. So Mercury's day is twice as long as its year.

Mercury turns on its axis with a steady speed, but its orbit is lopsided. When it is nearer the Sun, it moves faster. For that reason, the Sun moves unevenly in Mercury's sky. From certain places on Mercury, you might see the Sun rise, then set (as though it had changed its mind), and then rise again. The same is true for sunset – first the Sun might set, then rise briefly, then set again.

*Left:* In this illustration, the bright yellow area of Mercury's tipped, lopsided orbit lies above Earth's orbital plane (*shown in blue*). The pink area lies below Earth's orbital plane. A red line shows the 7° tilt between the two orbital planes.

**Mercury — why the wacky orbit?**

Mercury's orbit is more elliptical, or lopsided, than any planetary orbit except Pluto's. Mercury's orbit is also more tipped against the general plane of planetary orbits than any orbit except Pluto's. Since Mercury is so near the Sun, you would expect its orbit to be nearly circular and in the plane of the Sun's equator, like the orbit of Venus. Why isn't this so in Mercury's case? Scientists do not know.

Space suits on Mercury would have to withstand extreme heat and cold on a planet bathed in bright sunlight and deep shadows.

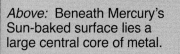

*Above:* Beneath Mercury's Sun-baked surface lies a large central core of metal.

*Inset:* Mercury was probably formed from rock and metal fragments.

# Metallic Mercury

When our Solar System came into being, the material outside the Sun turned into numerous small bodies. These small bodies gradually crashed into each other and formed larger bodies. The gravitational pull of the larger bodies attracted most of the remaining small bodies, and the planets formed. Like Venus and Earth, Mercury ended up with a large metallic core. Of all the known planets in our Solar System, Mercury's metallic core seems to be the largest for its overall size. Overall, Mercury is denser than the other planets. This means it is made up mainly of heavy rocks and metal with relatively little light material. There may have been more light material in the beginning, but if so, scientists are not sure what happened to it. Perhaps it boiled away because Mercury is so close to the Sun. Perhaps a large object hit Mercury and blasted the light material into space.

## Magnetic Mercury?

Earth and the four giant planets each have a global magnetic field. To have such a magnetic field, a planet must have a liquid core that conducts electricity, and it must rotate swiftly so that it sets the liquid swirling. The Moon and Mars do not have liquid cores, so they lack a global magnetic field. Mercury rotates very slowly, and scientists for a long time thought it was too small to have a liquid core. They believed it should not have a magnetic field, but it does. It has a weak magnetic field, and astronomers are not certain why. Perhaps it has a liquid or partially liquid core after all.

# Cratered Mercury

When a world forms, the last few bits of matter that strike it leave huge craters. Later on, additional sizable objects may occasionally hit the world, also creating craters. If the world is like Earth, its water and atmosphere wear down these craters and make most of them disappear. If the world has a lot of volcanic action, lava from the volcanoes covers the surface and, again, most craters disappear.

Small worlds like Mercury usually have little or no atmosphere and may not have much volcanic activity, so the marks left by the collisions tend to remain. Many visible craters exist on Earth's Moon, for example. Mercury, meanwhile, is so hot that its surface remained soft for a long time. It is even more thickly covered with craters than the Moon.

Both Earth's Moon (*left*) and Mercury (*above*) show the scars of collisions. A site on the Moon called the Mare Orientale looks very much like a similar basin on Mercury.

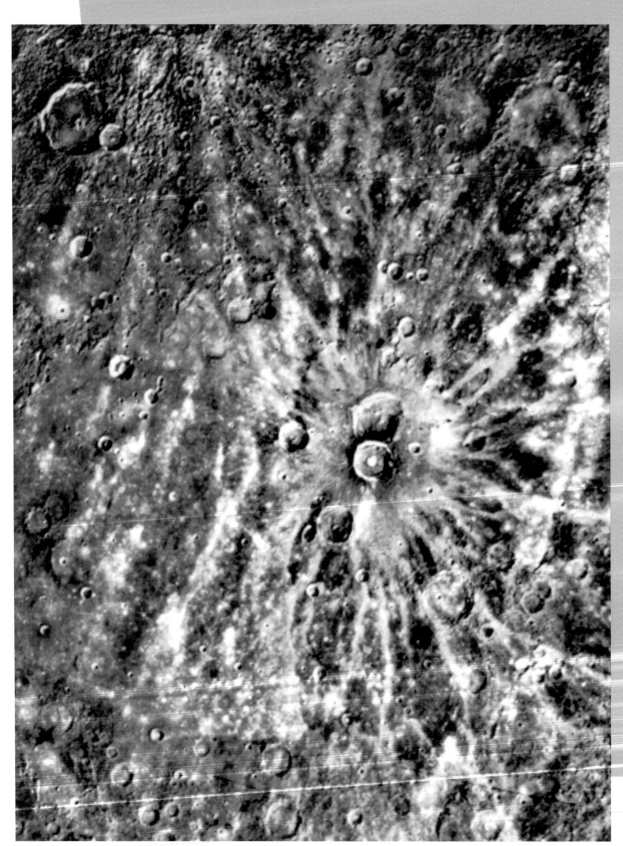

*Above*: This *Mariner 10* image shows the Degas crater with rays.

*Left*: The object that made Mercury's biggest crater, the Caloris Basin, also formed a series of circular ridges.

# Crater Caloris

If Mercury could be viewed from Earth as closely as our Moon can be viewed, it would look very much like the Moon. It is thickly covered with craters that look somewhat smaller than those on the Moon, but that is only because Mercury is a larger body, so its craters look smaller by comparison.

Mercury's largest crater is called the Caloris Basin. *Caloris* means "heat" – temperatures in the crater are among the highest on the planet. The basin is about 810 miles (1,300 km) across.

On Mercury, cliffs and fissures pass right across the craters. This may be because the planet shrank as it slowly cooled, and its surface cracked.

*Above:* An artist's conception of the Caloris impact.

# *Mariner* Visits Mercury

For centuries, Mercury was a mystery to Earthbound sky-watchers. In fact, until 1974, scientists knew almost nothing about Mercury's surface. All that could be seen through a telescope was a small body with vague shadows on it near the Sun. The planet went through phases, like the Moon and Venus.

In 1974-1975, a U.S. space probe, *Mariner 10*, changed our under-standing of Mercury. *Mariner* passed within 437 miles (704 km) of Mercury's surface. Then, as it went around the Sun, *Mariner* visited Mercury twice more, coming as close as 203 miles (327 km) to the planet. It sent back to Earth detailed pictures of almost half of Mercury's surface.

Most of what scientists know about the surface of Mercury comes from those pictures. No other craft has been sent to Mercury since.

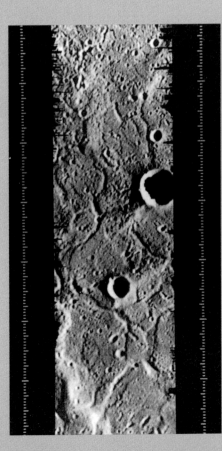 

Two views of Mercury.

*Left:* A rugged, cratered landscape.

*Right:* The cracked floor of the Caloris basin.

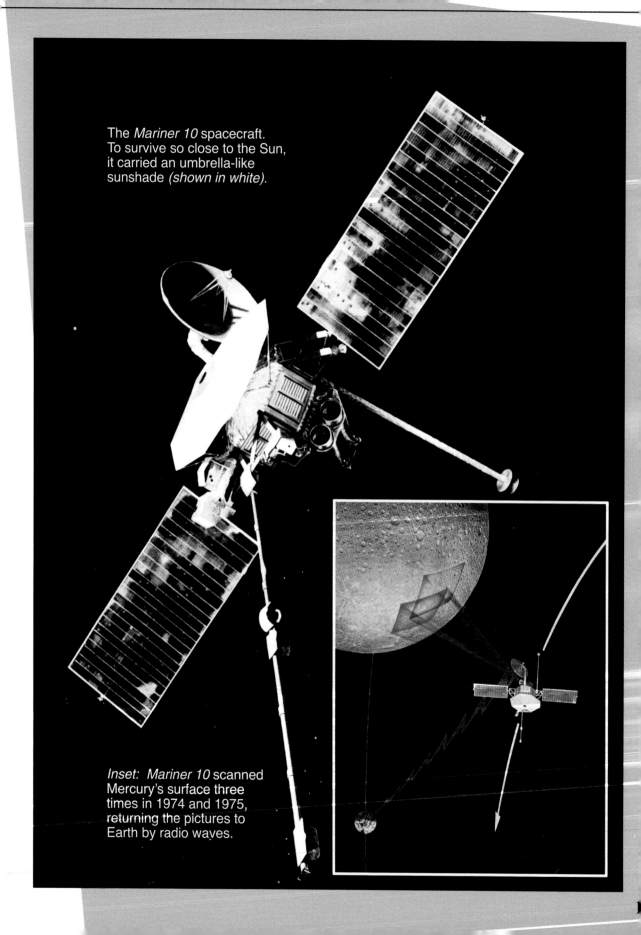

The *Mariner 10* spacecraft. To survive so close to the Sun, it carried an umbrella-like sunshade *(shown in white)*.

*Inset: Mariner 10* scanned Mercury's surface three times in 1974 and 1975, returning the pictures to Earth by radio waves.

Mercury's closeness to the Sun does not hinder observations from radio telescopes, such as the Arecibo telescope in Puerto Rico (above) and the Very Large Array (VLA) in New Mexico (*inset*).

# Ice on a Sun-baked World?

Mercury is certainly a Sun-baked planet, but some places on the planet are much hotter than others. Mercury's lopsided orbit, together with the relationship between its year and day, cause two areas along its equator to heat up much more than other parts of the planet. Astronomers refer to these locations as "hot poles." Whenever Mercury is closest to the Sun, one of these spots heats up to 850° F (450° C).

Even stranger, scientists believe they may have found ice on Mercury! In the 1990s, they beamed radar from radio telescopes on Earth to Mercury. The waves bounced off the planet's north and south polar regions and returned. Many large craters reflected the radar beam as well as icy moons in the outer Solar System do. Near Mercury's north and south poles, sunlight never shines into the floors of some craters — so it is possible that ice may lie hidden in them.

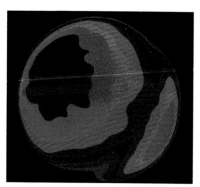

*Left:* The VLA radio telescope measured Mercury's temperature in order to create this map, which is shaded so that hotter areas are brighter. Mercury's "hot poles" can easily be seen.

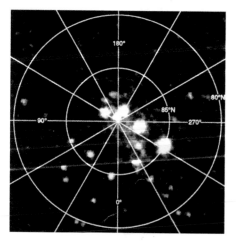

*Left and right:* By comparing radar maps with *Mariner 10* photographs of Mercury's polar regions, scientists find that the floors of many craters seem to reflect radar as well as ice does. Will future astronauts one day ice-skate on Mercury?

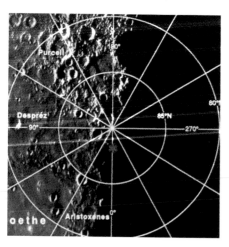

# Earth to Mercury

In earlier times, before space-crafts, astronomers could only see Mercury from Earth as a bright, starlike object. Of the five planets (not counting Earth) that can be seen without a telescope, Mercury was probably the last to be discovered. Even with a telescope, it looks small.

When Mercury is nearest Earth, the Sun is on the other side of it. During these times, Earth faces Mercury's nighttime surface, and the planet can only be seen from Earth as a tiny, dark disk as it crosses in front of the surface of the Sun.

When Mercury is on the other side of the Sun, its day side *could* be seen from Earth, except for one problem — the Sun hides it. Mercury can only be seen well from Earth when it is located to one side of the Sun. Then it is seen only as a tiny speck.

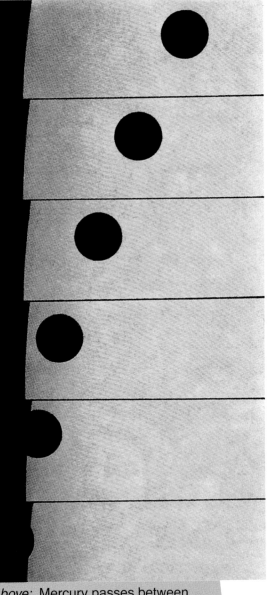

*Above:* Mercury passes between Earth and the Sun. These drawings are based on observations made in 1960.

The full disk of the Sun.
Mercury is the tiny black dot
near the bottom.

Mercury and the crescent
Moon. The entire disk of
the Moon is dimly visible,
illuminated by sunlight
reflected from Earth.

# At Twilight and Dawn

Mercury is closer to the Sun than Earth is, so we always see it quite close to the Sun. Look for it in the eastern sky just before sunrise, or in the western sky just after sunset.

In the evening, Mercury is visible for just under an hour or so after the Sun sets. At dawn, Mercury is in the sky up to just under an hour before the Sun rises. Of course, by the time the Sun rises, our view of Mercury is over.

To find Mercury, search for it in the twilight or the dawn.

*Left:* Polish astronomer Nicolaus Copernicus, the man who argued that the planets circled around the Sun.

## Looking for Mercury — to see or not to see?

Even around sunset or sunrise, Mercury is often so close to the Sun that it is hard to see. The sky is so bright just after sunset or just before sunrise that little Mercury can be missed. In 1543, Polish astronomer Nicolaus Copernicus explained that the planets circle the Sun, not Earth. Even Earth itself circles the Sun. Copernicus was one of the most famous astronomers ever, yet not once did even he manage to catch sight of Mercury.

# The Messenger Mercury

Most of the planets are named after ancient gods. Mercury, the messenger of the ancient Roman gods, is usually pictured with wings on his feet. These represent how rapidly he moved when he was carrying his messages. The planet Mercury moves across the sky more rapidly than the other planets, so it was named for this speedy messenger of the gods.

Metals were sometimes named for the gods, too. A certain metal looks like silver but is liquid. It was given the name *quicksilver*, which means "live silver." Quicksilver is also referred to as *mercury*, because of its "quickness." Mercury is the silver liquid in a thermometer.

*Below:* The metal mercury, or quicksilver, forms shiny liquid drops at room temperature.

*Above:* A 1961 NASA picture shows three Project *Mercury* astronauts in front of a Redstone rocket.

## Quick Mercury — fast and fooling the ancients

Ancient people believed that the faster an object moves across the sky, the nearer to Earth it must be. The Moon moves fastest of all, so it had to be closest to Earth. The ancients were right about that, but Mercury moves faster than Venus, so they thought Mercury was closer to Earth than Venus. We know that Mercury moves as fast as it does because it is near the Sun, not Earth. Venus's orbit is closer to Earth's orbit than Mercury's is.

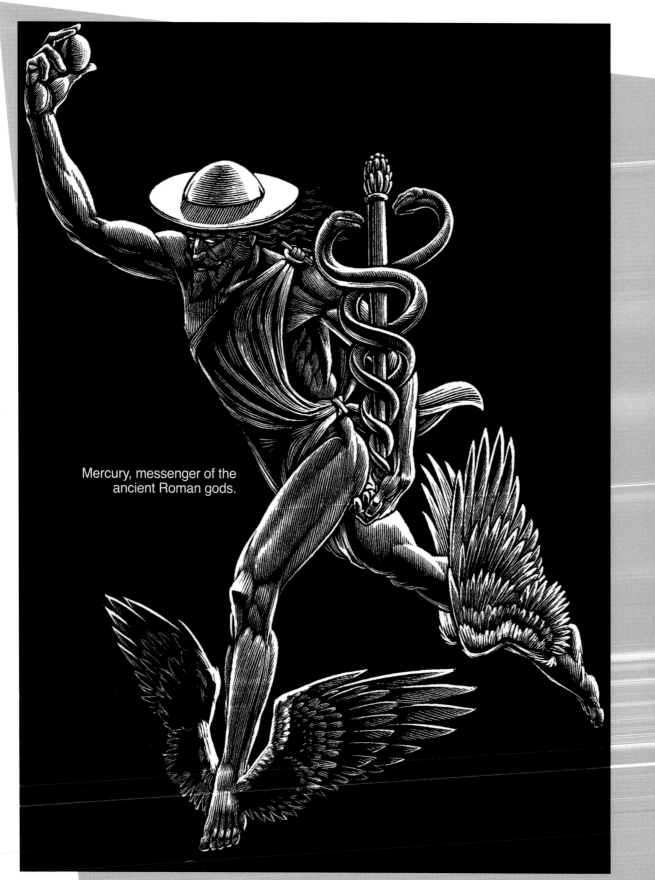

Mercury, messenger of the ancient Roman gods.

It was once thought that an unknown planet caused the odd motion of Mercury. The undiscovered planet was even given a name. It was called *Vulcan*, after the ancient Roman god of fire.

# The Odd Motion of Mercury

Mercury moves in its orbit because it is held by the Sun's gravity. The other planets also pull on it slightly. When scientists calculated all these gravitational pulls, however, it turned out that there was a tiny motion of Mercury that could not be explained.

Could this motion be caused by the pull of an undiscovered planet even closer to the Sun?

For a time, some scientists thought there might be such a planet. They called it *Vulcan*, after the ancient Roman god of fire. In more than 50 years of observation, however, astronomers never found this planet. Then scientist Albert Einstein presented a new theory of gravity — called the theory of relativity — that accounted for Mercury's odd motion.

*Above:* When a total solar eclipse occurred, it gave astronomers a perfect chance to see if there was an undiscovered planet closer to the Sun than Mercury.

*Above:* Albert Einstein, the scientist who explained Mercury's odd movements.

## Mercury's neighbors — getting an inside track on the Sun?

Some objects approach the Sun more closely than Mercury does. The asteroid 2000 $BD_{19}$ comes within about 8.6 million miles (13.8 million km) of the Sun, and some comets come even closer. If instruments could be placed near Mercury's poles where the Sun is always near the horizon and it may not be too hot, scientists could study these close approaches. They might even be able to study the Sun itself and get close-up answers to its many mysteries.

# Uncovering Mercury's Mysteries

*Mariner 10* mapped less than 1/2 of Mercury's surface, and many interesting discoveries remain to be made on the Sun's nearest planetary neighbor. Scientists would like to study the interior of Mercury and discover, for instance, if Mercury experiences earthquakes. It is possible that there are ice deposits deep within Mercury's polar craters. Studying the layers of ice will reveal much about Mercury's past. The ice might even help make it possible someday for humans to live and work on Mercury. The ice could supply water and oxygen for humans to survive, plus hydrogen that could be used as fuel.

The exploration of Mercury does not have to wait for a visit by humans in the distant future. Work is proceeding on two space probe missions that should tell scientists quite a lot about the planet. The U.S. space probe *Messenger* (the name stands for "MErcury Surface, Space ENvironment, GEochemistry and Ranging") is expected to go into orbit around the planet by 2009. The European Space Agency's spacecraft *BepiColombo* may arrive the following year. It will likely have two probes that will go into orbit and one that will land on the planet.

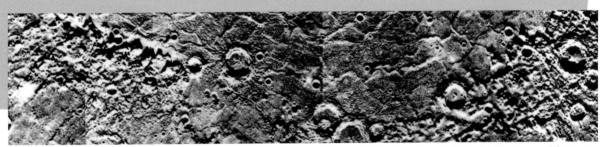

*Above:* The fractured Caloris Basin on Mercury.

**Tiny Mercury — small, but not a light-weight.**

We used to think Mercury was the smallest planet. Now we know Pluto is even smaller. Even so, Mercury is smaller than some moons. Jupiter's largest moon, Ganymede, and Saturn's largest moon, Titan, are both larger than Mercury.

Those moons seem to be made largely of icy material, however, while Mercury is made of rock and metal. If you could put worlds on a scale, Mercury would weigh more than twice as much as either of those large, icy satellites.

*Left:* As Mercury's interior cooled and shrank, its surface crust buckled and cracked — just as this apple's skin wrinkled as the apple dried out and shrank.

*Below:* An artist's conception of a spacecraft for the planned European Space Agency *BepiColombo* mission to Mercury later this decade. This shows the probe arriving at Mercury.

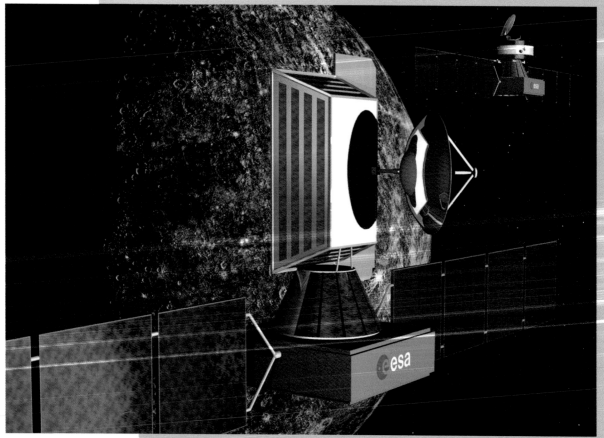

Mercury

*Left:* A close-up of Mercury. *Mariner 10* took photos that show Mercury's surface is even more heavily cratered than our Moon's.

## Mercury: How It Measures Up to Earth

| Planet | Diameter | Rotation Period | Period of Orbit around Sun (length of year) | Moons | Surface Gravity | Distance from Sun (nearest–farthest) | Least Time It Takes Light to Travel to Earth |
|---|---|---|---|---|---|---|---|
| **Mercury** | 3,032 miles (4,875 km) | 58.8 days* | 88.0 days | 0 | 0.38** | 28.6–43.4 million miles (46.0–69.8 million km) | 4.3 minutes |
| **Earth** | 7,927 miles (12,756 km) | 23 hours, 56 minutes | 365.256 days (1 year) | 1 | 1.00** | 91.3–94.4 million miles (147–152 million km) | — |

\* Mercury rotates, or spins on its axis, once every 58.8 days. It rotates three times for every two trips it makes around the Sun. Because Mercury rotates so slowly, the Sun stays up in Mercury's sky far longer than in Earth's sky. So from Mercury's surface, a solar "day" (sunrise to sunrise) lasts 176 days.

\*\* Multiply your weight by this number to find out how much you would weigh on this planet.

The Sun and its Solar System family (*left to right*): Mercury, Venus, Earth, Mars, Jupiter, Saturn, Uranus, Neptune, Pluto.

# Fact File: The "Quick" Planet

Mercury, the closest planet to the Sun, is the second-smallest known planet in our Solar System. Only Pluto is smaller. Mercury's atmosphere is very thin, so the planet has no real "weather" as we know it on Earth — only incredibly hot days and incredibly cold nights. Like Venus, Mercury has no moons.

Not much was known about Mercury until the 1960s and 1970s, because Mercury is so hard to see from Earth. Since the planet only appeared as a tiny speck that went through phases like the Moon, scientists did not know what Mercury's surface was like. Thanks to *Mariner 10* and other efforts to learn more about this planet, we now understand many things about Mercury that were once mysteries, but there is still a lot to learn about the "quick" planet.

Even if human beings visit Mercury one day in the future, not many would want to live there. By studying Mercury, however, we can learn about the history of our Solar System — including our own Earth.

## More Books about Mercury

*DK Space Encyclopedia.*  Nigel Henbest and Heather Couper (DK Publishing)

*Mercury.*  Robert Daily (Franklin Watts)

*Mercury.*  Seymour Simon (Mulberry)

*Mercury, Venus, Earth, and Mars.*  Gregory Vogt (Raintree Steck-Vaughn)

## CD-ROMs

*Exploring the Planets.*  (Cinegram)

## Web Sites

The Internet is a good place to get more information about Mercury.  The web sites listed here can help you learn about the most recent discoveries, as well as those made in the past.

**BepiColombo.**  sci.esa.int/home/bepicolombo/

**Mariner 10.**  www.jpl.nasa.gov/calendar/mariner10.html

**Messenger.**  messenger.jhuapl.edu

**Nine Planets.**  www.nineplanets.org/mercury.html

**Views of the Solar System.**  www.solarviews.com/eng/mercury.htm

**Windows to the Universe.**  www.windows.ucar.edu/tour/link=/mercury/mercury.html

## Places to Visit

Here are some museums and centers where you can find a variety of space exhibits.

**American Museum of Natural History**
Central Park West at 79th Street
New York, NY  10024

**Henry Crown Space Center**
Museum of Science and Industry
57th Street and Lake Shore Drive
Chicago, IL  60637

**National Air and Space Museum**
Smithsonian Institution
7th and Independence Avenue SW
Washington, DC  20560

**Odyssium**
11211  142nd Street
Edmonton, Alberta  T5M 4A1
Canada

**Scienceworks Museum**
2 Booker Street
Spotswood
Melbourne, Victoria  3015
Australia

**U.S. Space and Rocket Center**
1 Tranquility Base
Huntsville, AL  35807

# Glossary

**asteroids:** very small "planets." Hundreds of thousands of them exist in our Solar System. Most of them orbit the Sun between Mars and Jupiter, but many occur elsewhere.

**atmosphere:** the gases surrounding a planet, star, or moon.

**axis:** the imaginary straight line around which a planet, star, or moon turns or rotates.

**Copernicus, Nicolaus:** a Polish astronomer who was the first to argue that the Sun, not Earth, is the center of our Solar System and that the planets revolve around the Sun.

**crater:** a hole or pit caused by a volcanic explosion or the impact of a meteorite.

**Einstein, Albert:** a German-born U.S. scientist. His theory of relativity, explained, among other things, unusual motions in Mercury's orbit.

**elliptical:** shaped like an oval. Mercury's orbit around the Sun is more elliptical than that of any other planet except Pluto.

**fissure:** a long, narrow crack, as in a rock or cliff face.

**gravity:** the force that causes objects like the Sun and its planets to be attracted to one another.

**magnetic field:** a field or area around a planet, such as Earth, where magnetic force can be felt. Many scientists believe that planets with a global magnetic field usually have a core of melted iron. The magnetic field is caused by the planet's rotation, which makes the melted iron in the planet's core swirl. As a result, the planet is like a huge magnet. Mercury has a weak magnetic field.

***Mariner 10:*** a U.S. space probe that was launched in 1973 and made three close approaches to Mercury in 1974-1975, during which it collected much data about the planet and made a number of remarkable pictures.

**moon:** a small body in space that moves in an orbit around a larger body. A moon is said to be a satellite of the larger body.

**orbit:** the path that one celestial object follows as it circles or revolves around another.

**phases:** the periods when an object in space is partly or fully lit by the Sun. Like Earth's Moon, Mercury passes through phases as we watch it from Earth.

**planet:** one of the large bodies that revolve around a star like our Sun. Our Earth and Mercury are planets in our Solar System.

**pole:** either end of the axis around which a planet, moon, or star rotates.

**probe:** a craft that travels in space, studying celestial bodies and in some cases even landing on them.

**radio telescope:** an instrument that uses a radio receiver and antenna to see into space.

**rotate:** to turn or spin on an axis.

**Solar System:** the Sun with the planets and all the other bodies, such as the asteroids, that orbit the Sun.

**Sun:** our star and the provider of the energy that makes life possible on Earth.

# Index

Born in 1920, Isaac Asimov came to the United States as a young boy from his native Russia. As a young man, he was a student of biochemistry. In time, he became one of the most productive writers the world has ever known. His books cover a spectrum of topics, including science, history, language theory, fantasy, and science fiction. His brilliant imagination gained him the respect and admiration of adults and children alike. Sadly, Isaac Asimov died shortly after the publication of the first edition of *Isaac Asimov's Library of the Universe.*

The publishers wish to thank the following for permission to reproduce copyright material: front cover, 3, NASA; 4, NASA/JPL; 5, © Stan Christensen, Courtesy of Beloit Corporation; 6, © Julian Baum 1988; 7, © Pat Rawlings 1988; 8 (large), © Lynette Cook 1988; 8 (inset), © Dorothy Sigler Norton; 9, 10 (left), NASA; 10 (right), © Larry Ortiz; 11, National Space Science Data Center and the Team Leader, Prof. Bruce C. Murray; 12, NASA; 13, © Rick Sternbach; 14 (both), NASA; 15 (large), Jet Propulsion Laboratory; 15 (inset), NASA; 16 (large), Courtesy of NAIC; 16 (inset), Courtesy of NRAO/AUI; 17 (upper), Courtesy of Michael J. Ledlow; 17 (lower, both), Courtesy of *Sky & Telescope* Magazine; 18, 19, © Richard Baum 1988; 20, © Dennis Milon; 21, AIP Niels Bohr Library; 22 (left), Matthew Groshek/© Gareth Stevens, Inc.; 22 (right), National Space Science Data Center; 23, 24, © Keith Ward 1988; 25 (left), NASA; 25 (right), AIP Niels Bohr Library; 26, NASA; 27 (upper), The University of Chicago Library; 27 (lower), © 2001 ESA, Illustration by Medialab; 28, © Sally Bensusen 1988; 28-29, © Sally Bensusen 1987.